BRIGHT IDEA BOOKS

WOULD WE Survive AN ALIEN INVASION?

by Katie Chanez

CAPSTONE PRESS

a capstone imprint

Bright Idea Books are published by Capstone Press
1710 Roe Crest Drive, North Mankato, Minnesota 56003
www.mycapstone.com

Library of Congress Cataloging-in-Publication Data
Names: Chanez, Katie, author.
Title: Would we survive an alien invasion? / by Katie Chanez.
Description: North Mankato, Minnesota : Bright Idea Books are published by
  Capstone Press, [2020] | Series: Aliens | Includes bibliographical
  references and index.
Identifiers: LCCN 2018060989 (print) | LCCN 2019000040 (ebook) | ISBN
  9781543571189 (ebook) | ISBN 9781543571103 (hardcover) | ISBN 9781543574975 (pbk.)
Subjects: LCSH: Unidentified flying objects--Sightings and
  encounters--Juvenile literature. | Human-alien encounters--Juvenile
  literature. | Attack and defense (Military science)--Juvenile literature.
Classification: LCC TL789.2 (ebook) | LCC TL789.2 .C433 2020 (print) | DDC
  001.942--dc23
LC record available at https://lccn.loc.gov/2018060989

All internet sites appearing in back matter were available and accurate when this book was sent
to press.

Editorial Credits
Editor: Claire Vanden Branden
Designer: Becky Daum
Production Specialist: Melissa Martin

Photo Credits
iStockphoto: 3000ad, 9, 29, bertos, 21, 28, chainatp, 5, estt, 30–31, grandeduc, 14–15, gremlin,
24–25, Михаил Руденко, 18–19; NASA: PL-Caltech, 12–13; Shutterstock Images: 3000ad, cover,
26–27, Design Projects, 10–11, Fred Mantel, 6–7, Pavel Chagochki, 17, ra2studio, 23

Design Elements: Shutterstock Images, Red Line Editorial

Printed in the United States of America.
PA70

TABLE OF CONTENTS

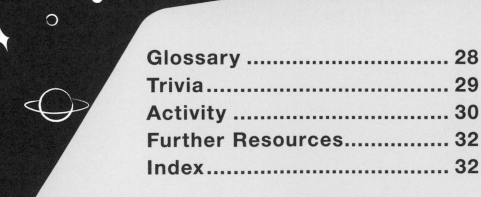

CHAPTER 1

A BIG Scare

People turned on their radios. It was a Sunday night in 1938. Televisions were not popular yet. People listened to radios for shows and the news.

The Sunday show started out like it did every week. Then it suddenly took a turn. A news reporter said **aliens** were **invading** Earth. People began to run for safety.

The radio show caused many people to panic. They believed aliens were going to attack them.

5

Many people want to have a plan in place in case aliens actually do invade Earth.

NO ATTACK

Highways became jammed with drivers trying to escape. People were crying. They thought they were going to die.

But there was no attack. It was just a **play**. The reporter was an actor named Orson Welles. The play was based on a book called *War of the Worlds*. Welles said he never meant to scare anyone. Earth was safe. But people started to wonder. What would happen if Earth was really attacked? Would we survive?

WAR OF THE WORLDS

H. G. Wells wrote *War of the Worlds*. It was published in 1898.

CHAPTER 2

WHY WOULD They Attack?

People have ideas on why aliens might attack. Some think they might want Earth's water. Others think they want to study people. They might want people as workers.

Earth's surface is about 71 percent water. Aliens might come to Earth because they have run out of water on their planet.

Aliens also might need a new place to live. They could have ruined their home. People have taken over other countries. They have started wars. Some think aliens could do the same.

Some people think aliens would want to take over the entire world.

11

Voyager 1 was launched in 1977. Its mission was to explore the edge of our **solar system**.

HOW WOULD THEY GET HERE?

Aliens would need spaceships to reach Earth. They would need better spaceships than humans have. Only two spacecraft from Earth have left our solar system. The first took 35 years. The second took 41 years. This spacecraft traveled far from Earth. It has traveled more than 11 billion miles (17.7 billion kilometers).

Aliens would have to travel many **light years**. One light year is almost 6 trillion miles (9.6 trillion km). Nothing on Earth is faster than the speed of light. Aliens would have to travel faster than light.

MILKY WAY

Earth is in the Milky Way galaxy. The Milky Way could be 200,000 light years wide.

Aliens would have to travel very far and very fast to reach Earth.

CHAPTER 3

WHO Wins?

Some people think we would lose the war against aliens. They could have better weapons. They could go after our computers. Computers run many army weapons. Aliens could turn our weapons against us.

Some people think aliens could easily take over the world.

17

Space suits protect
astronauts in outer space.

Others think people would win. Aliens come from far away. The air on Earth is different. People need special suits in space. Aliens might need them on Earth. They might die without them.

DEADLY BACTERIA

The aliens died in *War of the Worlds*. **Bacteria** on Earth made them sick.

People could also win by fighting.
Countries use armies to fight in wars
on Earth. Armies could be used to fight
aliens. Or we could not fight at all.
We could talk to the aliens to find peace.

Many people think
that we could be
friends with aliens
and live together on
Earth in peace.

CHAPTER 4

NO REASON to Be Afraid

Scientists have not found alien life yet. But there may be plans in place if they do attack.

Most government plans are secret. But many people think there is a basic plan in place. First the government would tell everyone to stay home. It would give orders over the TV or radio.

In an alien invasion emergency, the government might give information through newscasters on television.

BREAKING NEWS

Then the government would try to talk to the aliens. It would see if they are mean or friendly. We would find peace if the aliens were friendly. We would go to war if they were mean.

If aliens came to Earth, the government would need to be very careful when it makes contact. It wouldn't want to anger the aliens.

Alien invasions are still just ideas in science fiction movies for now.

But most scientists don't think we should be afraid. Aliens might be scared of people. We might reach them first. We could hurt them by accident.

Aliens might not even want to come to Earth. Do you think they will come someday? What do you think would happen if they did?

GLOSSARY

alien
a creature not from Earth

bacteria
tiny germs that can make
people or animals sick

galaxy
large groups of stars and
solar systems in the universe

light year
how far light can travel in one
year; a measurement used
in space

play
a performance of a story

solar system
the sun and the planets and
other bodies that revolve
around it

TRIVIA

1. Orson Welles became a famous movie director after his radio performance of *War of the Worlds* caused nationwide panic.

2. Many groups have tried to contact aliens. They have not received any messages so far.

3. The National Aeronautics and Space Administration (NASA) has a department called the Office of Planetary Protection. One of its jobs is to make sure bacteria is not accidentally spread between planets.

ACTIVITY

COME UP WITH YOUR OWN ALIEN INVASION!

Write a story or draw a comic about an alien invasion. Describe your aliens. Why are they attacking Earth? How are they attacking? Now switch to the humans. What are they doing to defend themselves?
Who wins? Why?

FURTHER RESOURCES

Want to know more about aliens? Learn more here:

Hoena, Blake. *Can You Survive an Alien Invasion? An Interactive Doomsday Adventure*. You Choose: Doomsday. North Mankato, Minn.: Capstone Press, 2016.

Hunter, Nick. *Have Aliens Visited Earth?* Top Secret! Chicago: Heinemann Raintree, 2016.

PBS Learning Media: Life Beyond the Solar System
https://tpt.pbslearningmedia.org/resource/nvfl.sci.space.beyond/life-beyond-the-solar-system

Curious about the science behind aliens? Check out these websites:

Environmental Education for Kids: Alien Invaders
http://eekwi.org/earth/aliens.htm

Universe Awareness: Alien Invasion Not Likely
https://www.unawe.org/kids/unawe1543

INDEX